A Burger Boy on Route 66

"Even God Loves Hamburgers!'

Written by Marty Hall

Authored and Designed by Lina Gilliland

Marty Hall

Marty Hall

ISBN-10:1981313265
ISBN-13: 978-1981313266

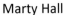
Marty Hall

DEDICATION

This book is dedicated to the memory of my mom and dad for their unconditional and selfless love which went far beyond raising me to the age of eighteen. They will always be remembered with great love.

This book is also dedicated to my wonderful wife and children, for their unfailing support and devotion which assisted in making my dream a reality.

Juanita Hall

Sidney Hall

Carolyn and Marty on their wedding day

Table of Contents

Andrew Zimmern with Marty and Carolyn Hall at Sid's Diner during a filming for the Travel Channel.

ACKNOWLEDGMENTS

I would like to personally acknowledge all the great people I have had the privilege of working with all these years. I have forged many lifelong friendships and learned many valuable lessons from every one of you!

To all the incredible customers that have passed through my doors and will continue to walk through in the future I thank you! Sid's Diner has become the warm well-known place it is because of all of you!

Lastly, I would like to thank Ms. Lina Gilliland for her hours of dedication in researching and assisting me with putting this labor of love together.

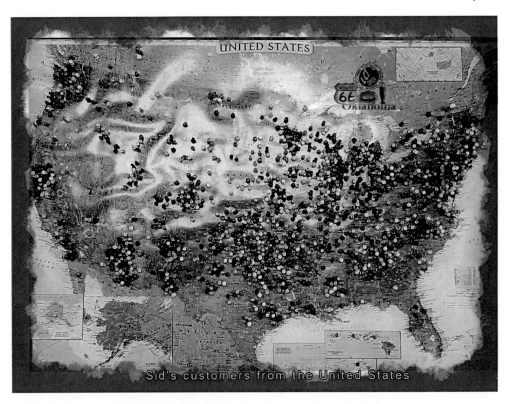

Sid's customers from the United States

Marty Hall with Andrew Zimmern and a local customer during a visit filming the Travel Channel.

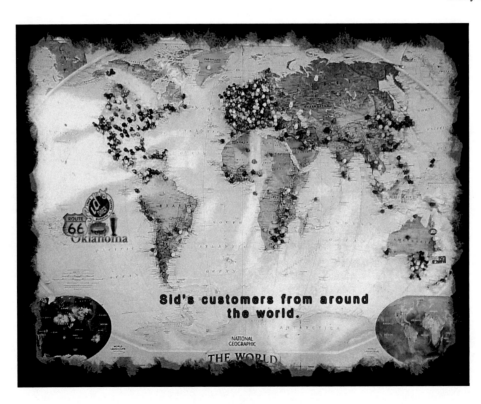

Here are a few comments from our customers over the years from around the world.

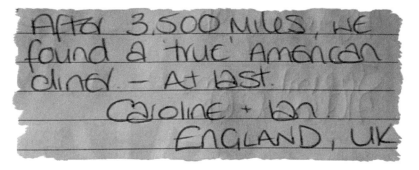

After 3,500 miles, we found a 'true' American diner. - At last. Caroline + Ian. ENGLAND, UK

We have placed several more throughout the book in gratitude for helping to make us what we are today!.

Cahills – Ashgrove Australia
(30 August 2008)
Best Burger in America?!?

n/8/08 Fergusons – Ashgrove AUSTRALIA
Milkshakes were good too.

FANTASTIC FOOD — THANK YOU
VERY MUCH FOR HOSTING US.
I LOVED THE PEANUT BUTTER /
BANANA SHAKE.
SID'S DINER ROUS.

SEBASTIAN   NEW YORK / BERLIN
TABEA   RAVENSBURG / GERMANY

1 INTRODUCTION

My name is Marty Hall. I am the owner of what is now known as a world-renowned hamburger joint called Sid's Diner home to the famous Onion Burger. Sid's is found in the small rural town of El Reno, Oklahoma located along historic Route 66, where at one time literally hundreds of Mom and Pop Diners could be found dotted across the United States.Most people are not aware that hamburger joints such as Sid's Diner were the precursor to today's fast-food chains. Now they are considered as much a part of Americana as fireworks on the Fourth of July.

Oklahoma is the birthplace of the hamburger on the bun. In 1993 Governor Frank Keating issued a proclamation which stated that the first true hamburger on a bun was created and consumed in Tulsa, Oklahoma in 1891.

Even though I built my dinner in 1990, I have been making hamburgers for more than fifty years. Sid's Diner, like many small diners located along Route 66, is a home away from home for many Americans in the towns in which they live. It is a place where kids grow up getting their first jobs, people come to mingle over a cup of coffee or stop in for their favorite meal with their family.

Diner's like mine have become a cultural American Icon. They are seen in paintings, films, novels, photographs, and museums in almost every facet of society.

Even Sid's Diner was featured in the movie Hollis. To this day they are known for having enjoyable food, reasonable prices, and relaxed down-home atmosphere.

On the set of the movie Hollis

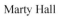

Marty Hall

Movie scene from Hollis featuring Sid's Diner

Marty Hall poses for a photo with the cast from the movie Hollis

.

One of the most enjoyable things for me in this business is talking with my customers, asking them why they chose to stop into Sid's Diner. The answers I have received over the years have amazed me. I have relished exchanging stories with them throughout all these years and yes, I remember every single one of them. My wife, Carolyn, has told me I need to write these stories down. Some extraordinary stories come from some of what would seem to be just ordinary people.

There were several major life events which happened to me along legendary Route 66 sometimes also called the Mother Road. Most recently, we were having a church service to honor the high school graduates, my granddaughter Breanna was among them. On that day we recognized their accomplishments, what their future plans were and at the end, we gave each of them the gift of a Bible.

Now I have attended several graduations in my lifetime and not one student to this day has ever stated they have wanted to flip burgers as part of their future. As a young man, it was also not in my future dreams to flip burgers for life either.

All my life and now as I stand here now at the age of 63 and reflect back over the years, I would not change a thing. The people I have met and all the incredible experiences I have had have been priceless!

That is what this book is about my struggles, my triumphs and my journey as a burger boy on Route 66. After all even God loves hamburgers!

A great way to start off our Route 66
road trip, amazing food & the
staff and customers are so friendly

THANKS!!

Hardy (Toronto, CANADA)
Dimitra (Athens, Greece)

1. FOND MEMORIES OF WAY BACK

I would like to start my story off by saying a few words about my ancestors. All of their hard work and dedication is the reason I am here today.

On my mother's side, my great-grandparents traveled out to Oklahoma from Arkansas by covered wagon. Oklahoma had just been decreed open to settlement by the Government; they were farmers and had heard the land was fertile to grow all sorts of crops.Back then Oklahoma was just-Oklahoma, a word that promised a better future for some.

It was not recognized as a territory and was not even close to becoming a state.

Their wagons were heavy and contained all the earthly possessions they owned. Weather-stained and muddy they eventually landed their wagon twenty miles west of El Reno.

My father's side was originally from Texas and settled in Southern Oklahoma. Eventually, they migrated from Southern Oklahoma to a place called Lookeba-Sickles, in what is now Caddo County, Oklahoma just a few miles South of Hinton.

Those days settling land was very hard. You had to be a mover! My families on both sides were no slackers to be sure. As the saying goes, "worked hard as the day is long." I have always admired them for their persistence and determination in raising their families

One of my favorite stories is about my great-grandfather, John Carlisle. I am telling the story as it has been passed down to me. John's office was the corner table of the Hinton Saloon and John well he liked to talk.

He was so good at it that he could buy a herd of cattle in the morning and sell them for a profit before the sun even set in the evening that's how good John was. I remember seeing him only once in my lifetime, he made an impression even then, that I did not forget.

The following picture is the only photograph I have of my great grandfather John Carlisle. It is placed on the bar countertop at Sid's Diner.

Marty Hall

Bonney and Boney

Now, my grandfather Boney Williams was the complete opposite of my great-grandfather Carlisle. He was a hard-working farmer and like great-grandpa Carlisle, I only remember seeing him once also. He was working the farm sitting high up on a tractor. People tell me that he was a very kind and generous man. Judging by my grandmother, I would have to say this must be the truth! My grandmother Bonnie was one of the most selfless, generous and finest women you could ever ask God to grace this earth with.

Marty Hall

One of the warmest memories I have of my grandmother Bonnie was when I was spending the night with her one summer. She had planned to fix chicken for supper that evening now these were the days that you didn't drive to the supermarket and pick up a package of chicken! No, I watched my grandmother gingerly walk out, open the chicken coop door and scoop up her intended target by its two legs! With the speed of light, she then proceeded to chop its head off, pluck its feathers and in one fell swoop it was on the dinner table. We were now eating it for supper, like magic before my eyes that was the best chicken I have ever eaten to this day in my life.

When my grandfather Hall grew up, he opened a store just eight miles south of Hinton. My grandfather and grandmother Hall worked hard in that store. I learned many good lessons from watching them. Some of my fondest childhood memories were staying with them.

In retrospect, I guess you can say entrepreneurship is in our blood.

Even though my parents didn't live all that far away from each other, they did not live all that close either. In all the years growing up, they had never crossed each other's paths until that fateful day each one decided to go to the Hinton Skating Rink.

My dad told me the minute he laid eyes on my mom, he fell in love, for him it was love at first sight and he never looked back. As young men do, he wanted to get her attention, so in trying to impress her he firmly put his hands in his pockets and began to skate backward.

However, something happened that even my dad couldn't explain and he went crashing to the ground. Everything in his pockets went flying and lay scattered all over the floor of the Hinton Skating Rink!

My mom said it left a definite impression on her.

In fact, so much so that about a year later they married.

During this time the Korean War was going on, the 1950's, and the war was in full force. My parents had not been married very long when my dad had just obtained his draft notice to report to the Army. My mother had just given my dad the news that she was two months pregnant with me when my dad had to leave.

My dad boarded the train station in El Reno, which is now our town's museum. My aunt told me that it was incredibly difficult for my mom to watch my dad leave that day, she cried and cried.

El Reno Train Depot

To this day when I go to visit the El Reno Museum, I feel I can still hear my mom crying.

Marty Hall

Sidney Hall

My mom decided to stay with her family at the farm while my dad was away in the war. Since my dad was in the military my mom had access to the military healthcare system. The closest hospital was Tinker Airforce Base, east of Oklahoma City, which is about an hour one way. My mom always told me that I was nearly born on Route 66. She was having labor pains that morning, my grandparents decided to put her in the car and they drove her to Tinker Air Force Base. After spending nearly all day there, the doctors decided that on that day I was not going to be coming into this world and sent my mom back home.

Once everyone reached home sometime around ten O'clock on May 7th her water broke! For those of you who are not familiar with Oklahoma weather, May is a month which has a lot of bad weather and is one of our highest months for tornadoes.

So once again my grandparents put my mom in the back seat of the 48 Ford and headed down Route 66 to Tinker. Somewhere along that dark stretch of highway that evening they got caught up in a storm.

According to mom, this was not just any storm but this was a really, really bad storm. The night was darker than usual with the clouds wrapped in strong winds, lightning, and rain mixed with hail. The storm became so strong they had to pull off the road rather than risk an accident.

After waiting out the storm with the wind rocking the car to and fro they finally started the car. Eventually, they made it to Tinker and I was born at eight O'clock the next morning.

Juanita Hall with Marty Hall as a baby.

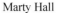
Marty Hall

I was eight months old when my dad returned from the war in Korea. The whole family showed up at the El Reno bus station. There the family eagerly waited alongside other families for the bus to show up. People remember the bus station being filled with emotion as the bus finally pulled up.

My mom recalled how all the servicemen had their noses pressed tightly up against the glass on the windows as they excitedly searched the crowd looking for their loved ones. Many who, like my dad, had children that were born while they were overseas. When my dad came off the bus, my mom handed me to him and she said there was not a dry eye anywhere. I am so thankful that my dad came home. Many soldiers did not, including 601 Oklahomans who died in Korea.

I recall coming home from school one day I was about fourteen years old. When I opened the door, a box full of letters was sitting there and each one of the envelopes had red and blue edging around it so I asked my mother about them. She told me that my dad was going to take care of them. Nothing more was said that day.

Then I was at my dad's funeral when out of the blue, one of my great-aunts handed me a letter. It was a letter my dad had written to her while he was in Korea. It was still in the original envelope, and to this day I still have it, I put it in a glass frame on the wall. So, after receiving this letter I became curious and asked my mom if my dad had ever written her any letters. My mom told me that she wrote to my dad every single day and that she got letters from my dad as well. I asked her where those letters were since of course I wanted to read them. She told me that my dad had burned them. In amazement, I looked at her and asked why- not comprehending how you could destroy those memories.

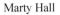

She looked at me and then said there were things in those letters that were only between me and your father and then understood...

CUSTOMERS VISIT
FROM JAPAN AND
KOREA

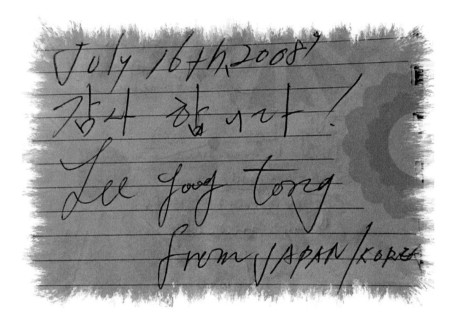

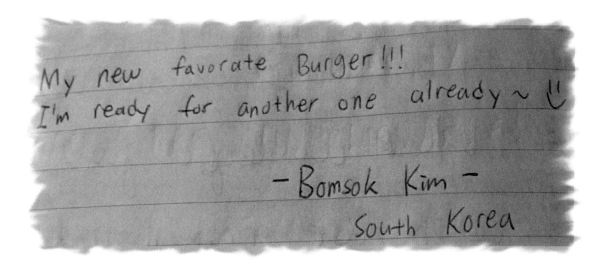

My new favorate Burger!!!
I'm ready for another one already ~ ☺

- Bomsok Kim -
South Korea

CUSTOMER VISITS FROM SOUTH KOREA

2 EARLY YEARS, FUN AND TROUBLE

My dad and mom decided to move to Houston when I was a year old. The economy was good; my dad was hired at the local Folgers Coffee plant. Then we moved to the nearby town of Pasadena, Texas. We had decided to go visit my grandmother in Jacinto City, that particular day family had come down from Oklahoma. I had a cousin who was about the same age as I was, which at that time, was six years old. We were playing and talking when he asked me where I lived. Too young to give him directions I told him

I would show him instead. Dressed in our cowboy hats, chaps, and boots and armed with the best cowboy guns known to a six-year-old we started walking to my house. Well, my house was over ten miles away! We walked about a mile down this two-lane blacktop road when a police car pulls over.

The police officer looks at both of us and asks us where we were going, under the brim of my cowboy hat I told him we were going home to my house. He crossed his arms and asked, "Where is your house? "Not skipping a beat I replied, "Pasadena." "Do your parents know where you're at?" "I forgot to tell them." I knew I was in trouble then and my cousin was not going to help me.

The officer then told us to get into the back seat of the police car. Both of us crawled into the back seat of that car. The door slammed shut, we knew not to say a word or we would end up in jail for sure! The police officer drove us back to my grandparent's house and knocked on the door.

It was my mother that came to the screen door, I was frozen with fear, I can still remember the wide-eyed expression on her face. A long pause filled the air then police officer looked at my mom and asked," Does he belong to you?"

Suddenly, my cousin had become invisible as all eyes became fixated on me. Nodding her head with purpose only a mother has, she replied yes with a mixture of fear and relief in her voice. That police officer wasted no time in telling my mother exactly what my cousin and I was doing a mile down the road. Now the whole family had gathered around, behind and on the side of that screen door. As I recall, there was enough upset at the two of us, we were in trouble any which way we turned. The first time I was ever arrested was when I was six years old!

My parents decided we needed to visit my grandparents in El Reno. They lived on the southwest corner of Old Highway 81 and Route 66. Dad and I were watching my grandfather work on a tractor. We had been out there a while, so nature was calling me, I turned and told my dad I needed to use the restroom.

At this time my grandparents did not have indoor plumbing. They still used a small outhouse for those things. So my dad looked at me and told me to go over to that little house and use the restroom. While I was in there, I noticed a box of matches lying there. It was just too much temptation for me! I had to open that box and look at those matches with that crisp red tip calling Martttyyy.

So one by one I started lighting each match. Then I would throw them down the hole in the outhouse. It went fine for the first minute, minute and a half but when the second minute hit…

Boom! The outhouse was on fire. I don't remember my legs ever running so fast as I ran out the door to tell my dad. We watched as our facilities burnt to the ground and a pile of gray ashes was all that stood in its place. Now looking back, I put an appalling amount of gray hairs on the heads of my family members. Through everything, they still loved me anyway.

Thirteen was a turning point in my life. Without even realizing what was going on behind the scenes this would be the start of my life path. My parents began talking about moving back to Oklahoma. Thirteen is a big time in any child's life but most especially a boy. He is no longer a little kid and he is not a man either which makes moving to a new state especially hard.

I wanted my parents to know I did not like this idea, not only did I not like the idea but I hated the idea! I gave them a really bad time.

After all, this was my whole world. All my friends were here I had just been picked to play on a Texas All-Star Baseball Team and I felt like I had the world at my fingertips. It was my dad after all that had taught me how to pitch. Now on some whim, I was losing everything to move to El Reno!

3 HARD DECISIONS

I did not get to play on the team that year. We moved to El Reno and ended up living in my grandmother's one-bedroom rent house. I was the oldest in the family then came two sisters and one other brother. My parents, of course, had the bedroom with my brother and sisters sleeping in the living room and I had a cot in the kitchen. I hated moving from my beloved home in Texas but even more, I detested El Reno!

There were not enough words in my vocabulary to let my parents know how much I loathed this desolate, dusty, nowhere place.

My mother's brother, my Uncle Butch intervened he took me to Johnnie's Grill to apply for a job. Otis Bruce was the owner. Otis looked me over and asked me if I was interested in a job except back in those days men talked to you like a grown up and expected you to answer like one! I had never applied for a job before which made me pretty nervous I looked down at the floor and shrugged my shoulders. My response was obviously not what Otis wanted to hear since he told me if he ever needed me he would give me a call and continued on with his day. Johnnie's Grill sits right on Route 66 and is still open today.

One of the main reasons we moved back to Oklahoma was that it had become hard for my dad to find work after the Folgers Coffee Plant had been shut down. At the time, being the age I was, I did not understand all the decisions my parents had to make until I grew up and started having my own family. There was one night in particular that changed my life. My dad had a friend named Max who owned a local grocery store.

I was unaware at the time that Max had been allowing my dad to charge our groceries until that night when my dad had come home late.

I could tell by the way my dad was talking that he obviously thought I was asleep. He and my mother were sitting at our dining room table across from each other my dad with a combination of worry and helplessness in his voice and my mother with an equal amount of concern to match.

I could tell just by the tone of my dad's voice he had reached the end of his rope as he was explaining what had just happened to my mom. He told my mom that he had just come from the grocery store since he knew we were out of food. He went in and picked out the groceries, as usual, nothing extra just the basics to get us by.

When he got up to the cashiers, however, Max was not there it was someone else he didn't know. My dad went on to say that the lady who was working that night would not let him charge the groceries so my dad had to go back and put everything on the shelves. At this point, my dad's voice was trembling and my mom was holding his hand trying to give him some comfort.

With acute clarity, I recollect laying on my cot in the kitchen and looking up at the ceiling hearing the distress in my parent's voice. It was then that I said to myself Marty you have to grow up. The next morning I got myself up, cleaned up and put on my good clothes.

I was unwavering I was going to help my family. I walked down to Johnnie's Grill on Route 66 placed my hand on the doorknob, this time I wasn't the nervous kid when I walked in.

Marty and Otis

I walked up to Ottis extended my hand, looked him in the eye and told him I indeed wanted a job working in his restaurant! I stood as straight as I could then asked him politely to please give me a job.

Otis Bruce did just that he hired me that day. The first thing he had me do was peeling onions. I had never peeled onions in my life! Twenty-five pounds of onions sat before me, my eyes never burned, stung or teared up so much in my life.

We sliced them on a razor-sharp mandolin with all the tearing my eyes were doing I ended up slicing my hand that day. That was just part of the job as a burger flipper something you took in stride and didn't grumble about. The following day was easier I was told my duty for that day was to keep the dishes washed.

This was during the last week of July and the temperatures were reaching the triple digits. We had gas burners going under the sinks in order to keep the water hot so you can imagine how warm it would get during those summer months!

The only thing we had to cool us off was a fan there was no air conditioning but then growing up that way we actually didn't know the difference and kept right on working.

Glenn was one of the boys who worked there. He walked up to me while I was working with a six-ounce Dr. Pepper. He handed it to me and said, "Here kid you look like you need this."

The taste of that Dr. Pepper was the unsurpassed! The best that ever went down my throat! Some things in life you can still feel and taste like they were yesterday this was one of those.

My throat was so parched and soaked in sweat from the heat of the summer that when that sweet syrup and icy coldness hit the back of my throat I was immediately cooled down by twenty degrees. Life was great the rest of the day!

On my third day, I had to work the night shift-I was gaining experience quick!

It was myself and two other boys working that night. Chris was the cook and Malcolm was his friend who worked at the filling station across the street. Being no stranger to mischief, you would have thought I would have known right away that something was up when they appeared in the back room while I was washing the dishes with these Cheshire cat grins on their faces!

Nope, I wasn't paying any attention, before I knew it Chris and Malcolm were trying to put my head in the dishwater! I was fighting with everything I had in me. I was cussing, yelling, kicking and my arms were flying every which way. The plumbing in the sink was now leaking from where they had dunked my head in the sink.

I found out later this was part of being initiated into working there when you reached the age of being responsible for taking on the night shift. For me, that was seventeen years old. Some nights I would come into Johnnie's Grill and a new boy would be at work.

I knew the guy from the night before didn't pass the initiation. When the seasoned boys walked up to you, they would tell you,"You can do this the easy way or you can do this the hard way." Really what this translated into meant you had three choices, they could put your head in the sink, you could put your head in the sink, or you could just leave.

We had one or two that would just leave then there were one or two that would fight and have to have their heads dunked in the sink like me. The rest they just walked over and put their heads right down in the sink.

About two weeks after I had started working at Johnnie's it was near to closing time, while I was washing dishes in the back I heard the three men arguing. Before I knew it Chris was telling me to call the police the guys at the grill were fighting with each other. I picked up the telephone and dialed the police department. It just so happened that they had a car in the area said the dispatcher and would be there straight away.

Sure enough, the police car pulled up and an officer came into Johnnie's Grill. The officer told all three men to step outside and he wasn't asking them nicely either. All four of the men walked outside.

I thought to myself good now they will all go to jail! To my amazement, this was not what happened at all. One of the men swung open the diner door and walked back inside the restaurant. Chris and I stood there like two statues. "Who called the police?" the man's voice was like a hammer hitting glass and brought me out of my dazed state. Before I could process anything I heard Chris say,"That kid in the back" and he is pointing straight at me!This man tells me he wants to talk to me and I already know this can't be a good thing for me. I poke my head out from around the corner and look at him straight in the face to see what is going to happen. He points his finger at me and in a low determined voice tells me," Before this night is over I'm going to cut you up, kid!" Then leaves the diner.

By now I am terrified to walk out that door into the dark. I am certain my body is going to be all over the alley when daylight comes. So Otis and Chris decide to make sure and get me home safely that night. After some time had passed, this man started coming back into Johnnie's Grill to eat. Every time I would see him I would head straight for the back until he left.

When I opened Sid's Diner I still never said anything to this man. He would come in and eat breakfast in the mornings, he was a different man than he was back then. Time and circumstances had changed him. This man who sat at my counter was a kinder and gentler man, however, the episode from so many years ago had never left my mind.

He came in one morning for his usual breakfast

Sid's was not very crowded so I took the opportunity, put my spatula down, washed my hands and walked around the grill.

I sat down at the empty barstool beside him and shook his hand.

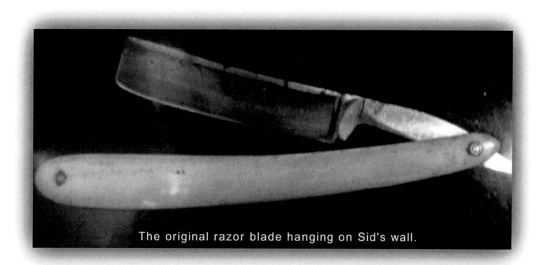

The original razor blade hanging on Sid's wall.

I then asked him if he remembered that night and shook his head and replied yes.

He looked at me and asked, "Was that you?" "Yes," I said. He apologized to me for what he said all those years ago.

He showed up for breakfast the next morning bringing with him his first razor and a picture. The picture was of him giving a little boy a haircut. We ended up becoming good friends, actually, he became a very close friend.

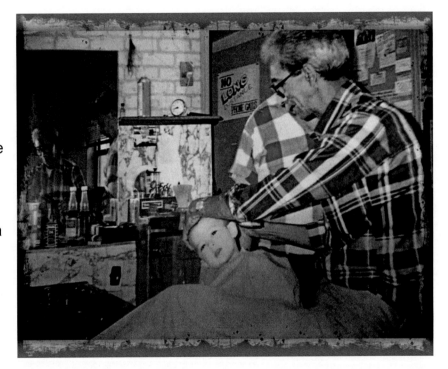

4 WHAT KIRBY TAUGHT ME ABOUT LIFE

After some time working at Johnnie's, I began to know most of the customers that would come in on a regular basis. There was one old man by the name of Kirby Phillips. Kirby was around ninety years old he was on the quiet side, had a tendency to be grumpy and had to have friends or family take him to Johnnie's so he could eat. I had just bought my first motorcycle and I was hot!

I don't recall the exact day Kirby called up to the grill and asked for me but what I do remember is that he told me he was not feeling very well and asked if I could bring him something to eat.

I packaged up some of Kirby's favorite food jumped on my motorcycle and rode to Kirby's house. I pulled up with a bag full of hot food and knocked on Kirby's door. Kirby answered the door and invited me to come inside. I walked inside and handed Kirby his food. I sat down in the chair so Kirby and I could talk. In those days you were polite. Kirby asked me about my family, how I liked working at Johnnie's and I, in turn, was able to get to know a little more about Kirby's life.

For the next three days, I took Kirby something to eat we would sit and talk. It wasn't too many days after that Kirby was feeling well enough to come into the grill. He came in one afternoon and after sitting down on the bar stool pointed his finger at me and said, "Marty come over here." I went over and stood across from him.

He opened his suit jacket and pulled out a gun laying it out on the counter between him and me. Kirby went on to tell me that he wanted me to have this gun, that he was one of the first police officers in El Reno and that this had been his gun.

Kirby's Pistol

I stood there not really knowing what to say. As I said thank you this means a lot to me, the words seemed inadequate for such a gift.

That day, Kirby taught me what giving a little of your time can mean to another human being.

Kirby also gave me the holster that went with that gun.

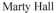

It was not long after that Kirby passed away. Kirby is someone I will never forget. I started to make a plaque for his gun with the intention of giving it to the museum. Many of the people around town that knew about the story advised me that I might want to rethink that. Those that knew me told me the gun would end up being put out of sight somewhere so it would be better off with me where Kirby wanted it.

Kirby at the barber shop

Kirby Phillips one of the first police officers of El Reno.

Many things had taken place during my first year at Johnnie's. I had grown up quite a bit from that whiny kid back in Texas. I learned some valuable lifelong lessons and made lasting friendships in El Reno. Otis had more business than his diner could handle so he decided it was time to expand. He moved the wall farther back, added three more barstools and got the latest sensation to the diner scene –a French fryer! Otis sent me to the J.W. Grill in Chickasha so I could learn how to make French fries from Richard.

French fries were a big deal for El Reno and people in town were ready to have those fries with their onion burgers. Off I went to Chickasha and met with Richard so he could show me how to make French fries. I arrived and opened the door to this small red and white burger joint. It had a few bar stools in front of the grill like Johnnie's with the cook flipping burgers and talking to the locals.

Richard shook my hand we exchanged hello's and went straight to the back. J.W. Grill had a potato peeling machine you would turn the machine on which turned this big barrel.

The barrel itself looked like concrete the inside of the barrel would spin then you would throw the potatoes in. You would drop the potatoes in the machine the inside of the barrel would rotate knocking off the peeling. After this was all done, we then ran the peeled potatoes through the slicer to make French fries. I still make my French fries at Sid's this way even now.

I went to school and worked at Johnnie's. The teachers let me leave five minutes early so I could run down to the grill and get ready for the lunch hour. Otis made sure I worked on the grill during the lunch rush.
The kids from school packed in that tiny place till you could hardly breathe! On most days I would clean up walk back to school and eat my lunch along the way.

On a few occasions, when I returned to the classroom, a few of the girls told me to go and eat somewhere else. I remember looking over at them and telling them to shut up and they could just go and sit somewhere else. I was a real hit with the girls as you can see. Looking back I laugh at this now however, I wasn't laughing then.

Otis came up to me one afternoon and asked me to work for him so he could go to the funeral home. Now, I told him, my parents, they would not let me out of school without a really good excuse. Mr. Reed, the Dean of Boys, would have to give me permission.

Otis assured me he would take care of everything so I could work for him that day. The next morning I woke up, and on my way to school, I stopped by the grill to pick up the excuse Otis had expertly written out for me.

I get to school and walk into Mr. Reed's office handing him the excuse and sit down across from his desk waiting for his answer. I see him reading the note he looks at me then back down at the note with an expression that I fail to understand.

Looking back up at me with a very serious expression, Mr. Reed asked,"Marty, are you going to cook hamburgers all of your life?" "I don't know Mr. Reed," I replied back. "I just don't want to get a whippin." He said,"I'll let it go this time but don't do it again!"

I had and have a great deal of respect for Mr. Hub Reed. He taught me how to drive; he is the reason I wear a button-down shirt and collar with a pocket, always tuck my shirts in with a belt and my hair never gets long enough to touch my collar. I have a story about Hub a little further down in this book.
He had a significant impact on my life that served to shape the person I am. I am grateful to have had a person like him around.

A.J. MAININI, JACK PISAN, MAX TONETTI THE
NAU MAU, LAUREN BLONDE BOBR, DARI SILVY
DARK BOBR AND MARK THE AUDITOR
FROM NORTH OF ITALY (NEAR MILANO)

5 LESSONS FROM THE 1960'S AND 1970'S

The late 1960's and early 1970's were to be some of the most memorable times in current history. President John F. Kennedy had been shot in 1963 sending the Nation into a spiral. Medicare and Medicaid were implemented by Lyndon B. Johnson. The Civil Rights Act was created; Martin Luther King Jr. was assassinated, and the famous Woodstock event took place! In the early 1970's the Vietnam War ended; we had the infamous Watergate Scandal and President Richard Nixon resigned from office.

Marty Hall

Durning my teenage year's nothing was boring everything was exciting and everything was fast.Once I was finished with school or work I kept myself busy with muscle cars, street machines, and fast motorcycles. Cruising with other teenagers down old Route 66 just like a scene out of a movie.

We would meet up at a specific spot and cruise through Sonic, Jobes Drive-In to the Bowling Alley and back again. Laughing, joking having a great time with our bold muscle cars all shined up. It was a magnificent time to be a teenager. My Uncle Butch had an auto shop if I wasn't working at Johnnie's Grill I would be down at my Uncle's shop. I cleaned engine and transmission parts for cars.

My Uncle showed me how to disassemble and put engines back together to make them run right. I learned an immense amount from my Uncle Butch! My Uncle Butch wasn't just a mechanic. He was considered *the mechanic* for hot rods in El Reno! Anybody that was anyone in the Hot Rod business took their car to my Uncle Butch. His shop was always full of cool cars and guys talking about the latest edition of Hot Rod magazine.

I'll always be thankful for my Uncle Butch. He knew what I needed even when I didn't. He kept me busy and out of trouble at night after I got off work. He taught me analytical thinking even though I didn't know that's what I was learning. I learned how to take almost anything apart and put it back together so it ran right.

One night I walked into the shop and sitting there was a Marina Blue 1966 Chevy Nova SS. I had seen the car around town. I remember thinking to myself that is one of the most beautiful cars I have ever seen! My Uncle Butch walked up behind me and stood there for a moment both of us admiring the magnificence.

The grill, the roofline, and that sharp backend all seemed to draw me in just like a woman. For any of you reading this who are car enthusiast you surely know what I am talking about!

Uncrossing his arms my Uncle Butch tilted his head and said," how would you like to own that car?" I stood there staring at my Uncle Butch in a state of suspended animation. I found it hard to believe that someone like me could own a car like that.

I do not exactly recall the words that stumbled out of my mouth but yes must have been one of them.

That next Monday Uncle Butch and I went down to the bank. I was a mixture of excitement and nervousness as I walked in. The loan officer called us in and invited us to sit down.

He went through all the paperwork with me making sure I understood all the fine print. Once we had ironed out everything Uncle Butch agreed to cosign on the loan for me.

After that my Uncle took me out and taught me how to drive a four-speed. Much to my mother's dismay he also taught me how to drag race beginning from the starting line and speed shift the gears. Life couldn't get any better at that moment in time.

When I look back over my life, there are three men who played a very important role in shaping me, my dad, my Uncle Butch, and Otis Bruce. I am very thankful they took an active part in my life. They kept me out of trouble; they taught me how to be a man, how to stand up for myself, figure things out and gave me a good work ethic.

Uncle Butch and Aunt Pat

This Nova was one very fast car! It was a typical balmy, breezy night in Oklahoma and I had taken my Nova out cruising with my friend Leroy. We were cruising Yukon on Route 66 and decided to stop in at a place called Arrowhead Drive-In.

Leroy opens the door and gets out of my car. He starts walking around going from car to car and talking to all the different guys, all the while I am sitting there thinking to myself what the heck is he doing?

After a few minutes, Leroy comes back with two of the guys to my car. One of them walks up to my window he leans down and says," You sure have a nice car." I told him thanks he goes on and says,"Do those mag wheels make your car fast?" I didn't say anything.

"How about that tachometer does that make your car fast?" nodding his head toward the dashboard. Leroy jumped into the passenger's side and closed the door I turned to him and asked, "What's going on?" "I bet this guy twenty dollars you could outrun him," Leroy said.

I turned to the guy standing at my window and asked," Where do ya wanna go race?" He said,"Follow me." So we took off and headed East of Yukon along that stretch of Route 66 between Yukon and Bethany.

I looked up in my rearview mirror and it looked like every kid in Yukon was following us out there! We lined up and made a burnout. Whenever I would get ready to race anyone my mouth would become dry and the palms of my hands would start to sweat very bad. I had a policy of never letting anyone ride with me when I raced, mainly because I didn't want the weight in the car.

That night I let Leroy ride along for that street race. My competition's car looked like a 1970's, Nova big block automatic.

The sign was given we take off I outrun him at the turnaround point no contest my Nova wins the race.

Leroy stepped out of my car he walked over to collect his money as he turned around to start walking back towards my car the crowd of teenagers started throwing beer bottles at him. He started running jumps in my car and says," Let's go get em'."

"I am not going back to Yukon!" I snapped. I backed my car up went through Bethany, down to the interstate and drove myself home that way. It was a long time before I ever went back to Yukon!

Not too long before graduation, we had an event happen just North of El Reno, we dubbed it *The Great Train Robbery*. There were several El Reno boys down by the river on their way back home. They had to cross over the railroad tracks to get into town, however, the train had been stopped, so they were not able to get through.

The train had a couple of the boxcars which somehow the doors had been left open. on Refrigerators, washers, and dryers escaped from those boxcars and were laying on the ground next to the tracks.Leroy happened to be there. He and the other boys were arrested and had to go before the judge. The judge told them they had two choices, they could go to jail or go into the military.

Every eligible young man at that time had a draft card this was the height of the Vietnam

War. About a week later, a military recruiter came to the high school. I remember I was sitting in the front row staring at this Marine. He was the perfect picture of what a Marine should look like just off the poster. He pointed straight at me and said,"Boy, I looked just like you before I joined the Marines!" I said, "Where do I sign up?"

I was handed a packet of papers to take home with me. Since I was underage it was explained that I would have to have my parents signature before I could enlist.

I took the papers home and spoke with my mom and dad explaining to them this is what I had decided to do. Neither one of them said a word. I would periodically check to see if they had signed my papers. Since the time for me to hand them in was growing closer and closer as each day passed by.To my bewilderment, they still had not signed them.

When I started driving motorcycles and then cars my father told me if I ever came home drunk he would kick me out of the house. My dad was the type of man that he meant what he said and said what he meant. He also was only going to say it to you one time. There was no doubt in my mind that was exactly what he would do.

I remembered that there was going to be a beer party, just North of El Reno, for some of the boys who were shipping out. I had to work that night but I was going out there later on after work. I told my mom that she and my dad had to sign those papers! That night before I got off work my dad called up to Johnnie's he told me he was not signing those papers. I became really angry with him I told him with a great amount of emotion that he had to sign those papers. Then I paused and I asked him why I couldn't go.

He said,"Son you have no idea what you are asking for if they draft you then you need to go but don't ask for it." I was so mad I slammed the phone down.

That night after I got off work I went out to the beer party. I came home about three O'clock in the morning my dad opened the door to let me in.

I went to the bedroom and laid down on my bed everything began spinning. It felt like I was going down into the toilet. I never felt so sick in my life. I was hugging that toilet and throwing up for the rest of the night. I continued to be sick the whole rest of the next day. My mom was taking care of me wondering why I was sick.

My Dad, however, was sitting in his chair not saying a word. To this day I know that had I continued this behavior my dad would have put his foot down and kicked me out of the house. I have never been drunk since then and that was the first, last and only time. It only took me one time to realize how stupid this was and how merciful my dad was to me.

Leroy ended up being shipped out as part of his court stipulation. I received only one letter from him, in that letter he wrote something that stood out above everything else.

He wrote a line which read as follows: *you really needed to thank your daddy for not signing those papers.*

I reflected on what my friend wrote. I knew he had been right.

My dad was looking out for me and saving me from some very horrific experiences and quite possibly from never returning home to live the life I have come to love so much.

3/17/2012

We are stuck on these
onion burgers. There are
GREAT!

Fondly
The Brietlin's
Belle Plaine, Mn.

6 MOLLY MURPHY'S TO SALVATION

After high school graduation, I had decided to stay working at Johnnie's Grill when one afternoon two well-dressed men came walking in. They sat down on the bar stools and looked over the menu. I took their order and proceeded to fix what they wanted After the gentlemen had finished eating their order I spent some time talking with them, the older gentleman handed me his business card. The card read Bob Tayar, Molly Murphy's Resturant.

Right there on the spot, he offered me a job! He asked me to call him when I got off work. He was interested in hiring me as a kitchen manager for his restaurant. I agreed to meet Mr. Tayar there one evening after work. The other gentleman which accompanied Bob was Mr. Hank Kraft. Hank is now the COO of Hal Smith's Resturants based in Norman, Oklahoma. Hank and I have stayed friends all these years.

Molly Murphy's House of Fine Repute Resturant was quite the place to go and had a reputation all its own. People came from all over to have a good time, be part of an atmosphere that was almost theater like and enjoy some good food home cooked food. Molly Murphy's was more of an experience than just a diner.

There really wasn't anything quite like Molly's. The waiters and waitresses were dressed up in costumes of all sorts and rushing past me back and forth at a furious pace as I was being given the tour of Molly's Kitchen.

There was Dr.Spock, Rasputin, Cinderella, Groucho Marx, and too many others to even remember. They even had a disco bar!

This place was way over my head. I couldn't imagine going from Johnnie's Grill to Molly's restaurant! I told Mr.Tayar I was honored that he considered me for this position and had asked me to manage one of his restaurants but I would have to decline. Then he asked me if I would look at one of his Drive-In's located on Route 66.

It was named Bonaparte's Drive-In. Again, I agreed and went with Bob to look at his Drive-In this was much more suited to my personality and my speed. We came to an agreement and I was hired as a manager there where I worked from seven in the evening until four in the morning.

I worked at Bonaparte's but my heart was still at Johnnie's. I had started my work-life there, I learned so much there, and it was my community where I felt a part of everything that happened.

After about six months I picked up the phone and called Otis. I let him know that if he ever needed me to just give me a call that I really would like to have my job back. It wasn't too long after that conversation that Otis called me back and I was hired back working at Johnnie's Grill! I am grateful for the experience I had at Bonaparte's and everything I learned in running a business. My place was here in El Reno.

Working back at Johnnie's allowed me to participate in the car shows once again. Being in El Reno was easier on my car, my car always placed well and I really enjoyed all the people I was able to meet. I took home a trophy at every car show. It was either a first, second or third place trophy.

There was one show I went to that was promoted by Darrell Starbird. It was a large show with over 300 cars by the time the show ended. I won a third-place trophy in my class.

I have to admit I was disappointed because from my point of view I thought I should have won first place. I began to pick my things up to go home when they announced that they had one more award to give out. The MC continued to say the National Street Rod Association had sponsored one final award to give out.

It was awarded to *Marty Hall* when I heard my name over the intercom I was overwhelmed that I won this award!

Once I got home that night, I was in the garage with my car, I was thinking back on all the events that had unfolded that weekend and even that day. It is difficult to explain what happened that night. I had a job, a home, a wife, and a newborn baby girl. From the perspective of the outside world, I had everything that would symbolize success.

I found that even though there was nothing material missing, I had a sense that deep inside that there was something that was absent from my life, however, I could not put my finger on it. It was roughly two months later I had a strong desire to go and see the film The Greatest Story Ever Told it was a show about the Lord Jesus. Growing up as a boy my mom and dad would take me to church but I have to say I didn't like it much.

My mom and dad were God-fearing parents. I can tell you that my mom said many prayers for me over the years. There were a lot of nights I would come home late. When I would walk through that door at night there sat my mom waiting up for me to come home. When I would drive by churches something inside of me would say to me I am supposed to be inside of there. Even with that nagging internal voice, I never felt compelled to stop in.

It was not until the night I watched this movie that I understood for the first time in my entire life what a great sinner I was. It was truly what some would say was an epiphany. I do not remember exactly what the conversation was that I had with the Lord. I do remember that I asked the Lord Jesus to forgive me for the sins I had committed throughout my life to be the shepherd of my being and I would follow Him.

I can tell you that something profound happened in my life that night that drastically changed me. I now know that it was the Holy Spirit coming into my life; changing my thoughts, my desires, and my language. I wanted to know more about this great Savior. Christianity is not a religion. It is a personal relationship with the Lord of Heaven and Earth. I suddenly had this yearning to read the Word of God, to go to church and to be around God's people.

Ever since that day a change came over my life from deep within my soul.

I started living from that moment forward knowing that I had a great Shepherd who leads me and guides me on this path. It has not always been easy. I cannot say the way is always clear before my eyes nor that I have a perfect understanding of why. I can say most of it has been pretty difficult as a matter of fact! The Lord has given me peace of mind and assurance in my heart that He was with me on this journey. I pray whoever reads this book will also come to know the Lord Jesus in such a personal way.

Two years have passed by now in my life living in this small town of El Reno. To bring you up to speed my family has grown from one child to three! A new addition to my wife and I, beautiful twin daughters had joined us. Now, there were three precious little girls I had to take care of. All of which were under the age of three! Many of you reading this can relate being responsible for a family means making sacrifices.

I sold my beloved Nova to my Uncle Butch. He had it just about a year when he tore the third gear up in the transmission. I cringe every time I think about it. After that happened, he parked it in his garage then covered the car up with a blanket. That Nova has sat in that garage and it has not been started for over forty years.

Whenever I go over to his house, I still enjoy going into the garage. I open the car door and sit inside. I can smell the interior, touch the gear shift and my mind is flooded with memories of the old days. I just sit quietly for a while and smile to myself. Those were good times very good times indeed…

7 MY FIRST BURGER JOINT

Not too long after I sold my Nova, I went to work one morning Otis was talking to me about a little Drive-In not too far down from Johnnie's off of Sunset Dr. on Route 66 called the Dairy Hut. The owners were Charlie and Velma Johnson. They were asking twelve thousand dollars for both the equipment and the business. Otis went and spoke to them about me buying their business. I was 21 years old at the time.

I had only used one bank in my long life so far and had bought my first motorcycle, my cars, and furniture for my house there. My dad told me that if I had made all my payments on time I could probably borrow the money needed from the bank. So I went down to the bank and spoke to a banker named Eddie. I filled out the application he gave me and spoke to him about my situation. Eddie said he would call me the next day and let me know if I was approved. I was so excited to have my own business.

The phone rang the next day I had butterflies as I picked up the receiver. It was Eddie calling about my application. My excitement turned to disappointment when Eddie told me they could not give me the loan. All I could say was thank you. With a sinking feeling at the bottom of my stomach, I hung up the phone. I called my dad and told him that the bank had turned me down for the loan. He asked me why I said I didn't know.

.

My dad told me to meet him at another bank in town. My dad and I went in together and spoke to the banker. The banker told us that my dad would have to cosign on the note and then he would give me the three thousand dollars to get the business.

My dad cosigned on that note and I got the three thousand dollars! I could not believe my dad did that for me! Three thousand dollars was a lot of money back then. As we were walking out of the bank I thanked my dad so much for that favor. He looked over at me and replied,"I believe in you. Don't let me down." I never did either.

The Johnsons would close the Dairy Hut every winter from December until March. I this was a great idea! It was a small white and blue building with two small benches on either side.

A walk up window on the left side where you could place your order and another on the right side where you picked it up. Inside the Dairy Hut, there was no place to sit down. You would walk up to the window place your order and be given a number when your order was ready your number was called and you would pick your order up.

You could eat your food in your car, on a picnic table or take it home. I truly did like the Dairy Hut. It was a clean and simple concept. I had two wonderful ladies helping me in the beginning. My Aunt Pat, who was Uncle Butch's wife and Mable Dodd as well as the teenagers who worked there. I was sad to see the building torn down years ago to make a parking lot. With so many fond memories I wish the building was still standing there on Sunset Dr.

It was at the Dairy Hut that I also cooked the famous El Reno fried onion burger. I also cooked fresh cut fries and served ice cream.

There was one cone that was my favorite above all the rest. It was a dipped cone with a crunch put on it. I remember that cone tasting so good! Unfortunately, like many good things, I cannot find the crunch anywhere anymore so now it is just a good memory.

Over the course of three winters, I would close the Dairy Hut and go to work in the oil fields. After my third year of doing this, I decided that I wanted to see how the Dairy Hut would do staying open during the winter time.

My plan was to stay open day by day. If we had a bitterly cold day I would close up shop and stay home. My gamble paid off in spades! Even in the wintertime, I did just fine! People were coming in eating burgers and fries, drink malts and shakes. It was so successful the Dairy Hut stayed open year-round after that. I ended up owning the Dairy Hut for a total of thirteen years.

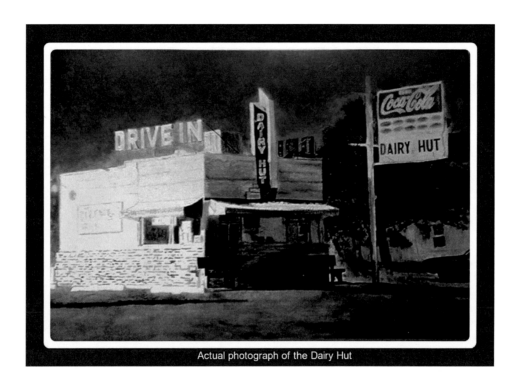

Actual photograph of the Dairy Hut

Marty Hall

8 FAMILY TRAGEDIES AND THE GIFT OF LIFE

I was driving through downtown El Reno one afternoon along Route 66, it was one of those cold Oklahoma days, the kind you only have in Oklahoma when I passed by a woman walking down the street. She was wearing a coat down to her ankles with the hood of her jacket pulled up over her head. That sure is one pretty woman I remembered thinking to myself. I drove around the block just to get another look at her!

I did some asking around and found out her name was Carolyn.

I managed to get her phone number and called her up. I wanted to see if she would go out on a date with me. She agreed to go out with me. Now remember I was not much of a ladies man, so I was taking advice from some of the girls who worked at the Dairy Hut. In their vast amount of wisdom, they were telling me that I was supposed to kiss her on the first date.

I picked up Carolyn and took her to a nice restaurant in Oklahoma City we then drove back to El Reno and out to the lake. I do not remember talking a whole lot when I looked at Carolyn and she was asleep! My thought was I must be a pretty boring guy if my date falls asleep. So I started my car and drove her home. On the way back I thought of what the girls at the Dairy Hut told me I should do. We got to her house I walked her up to the front door. I leaned in close my objective, of course, was to be able to kiss her.

Before I even had a chance she pushed me back hard with her hand and said goodnight. As I turned to leave I was thinking this was going to be the last date I would ever have with this lady. The next day she showed up at the Dairy Hut came in the back door and got something to eat. I could not have been more surprised!

So naturally, I asked her out on another date and we began dating. We got married six months later at a little church in Banner, Oklahoma which is just a stone's throw off of Route 66.

Carolyn has been very faithful to me. She has stood beside me all these years helping me raise our children, taking care of the house and taking care of me. I am so grateful that the Lord led me to her.

In 1982 our son Adam was born. Adam had been born two months premature weighing only two pounds and one ounce. Carolyn and I had gone to the doctor earlier that week since she was not feeling well. He had diagnosed Carolyn with toxemia poisoning. Some women develop this condition when there is too much stress put on their bodies.

We took her to Mercy Hospital where her doctor told her she was to lay as still as possible. She was not to cross her arms, her legs and lay only on her back. She did this for four days. On the fifth morning, the doctor came in the hospital room. It was still and quiet in the room. The type of quietness that comes before a storm when everything around you becomes a tunnel. She looked at us both. Solemnly she told us that she needed to take the baby that day if she did not Carolyn, my wife could possibly die. I looked at the doctor and asked her what chances the baby had of living.

She said she would give the baby a ten percent chance of living. I sat there in that room not knowing if I would lose the life of my wife or my child that day.

The nurses came in they carefully placed Carolyn on a gurney and wheeled her to the operating room. My mind and heart were filled with all the distress of a husband and a father together. I did the only thing I knew to do I went to the Chapel and I prayed. I begged the Lord to spare the life of my wife and child. While Carolyn was pregnant I would often place my hand on her stomach and say,"How is Adam today?" This was before the use of ultrasounds had become a standard clinical practice for finding out the sex of babies.

I did not seem to have been praying in that Chapel very long when John Kline opened the door and found me there. He came up beside me and asked, "What do you think of that little boy of yours?" I replied,"I didn't know I had a little boy." He also told me that my wife was fine and to come with him to see her.

Still, in a state of shock, I went with John. They were just bringing Carolyn out of the operating room and just as John had said she was fine. As soon as Adam was born the poison in her blood began to go away, however, what was happening was that her kidneys were failing due to the pregnancy. I went up to the nurse's station and asked one of the nurses where I could find my baby. She told me he was located up on the third floor in the prenatal unit.

I went up to the third floor found the prenatal unit. The nurses had me scrub down, put on a mask, gown and some gloves. They then brought Adam to me. An enormous needle had been placed in his head.

Softly I said,"Hi Adam," he opened his tiny eyes and looked at me. That was such an incredible moment in my life. A moment filled with more emotion than what could ever be contained with the walls of that hospital. I knew right then that everything would be alright.

Even though both Carolyn and I had insurance coverage when we got married our policy was clear that it did not cover maternity issues. Adam was in the hospital for two months. Every single day we went and saw him. The first thing every morning I would look to see how much weight he was gaining. The nurses had a scale right there where they would mark how many ounces he would gain or lose. The days he would lose an ounce would be a bad day but the days he would gain an ounce or even two were considered good days.

In the back of my mind though I knew I was going to have a large hospital bill. All I was going to do, the only thing I could do was to go down and set up a payment plan to pay so much money on the bill every month.

When I knew Adam was due to be released from the hospital I made a visit to the billing department the day before. I needed to see what I had to do as far as paying this bill.

I sat down and had a conversation with the lady that was dealing with our insurance company over these bills. She kindly explained to me that even though our insurance would not cover maternity issues it would cover all maternity-related complications.

My insurance had paid all the bills! Carolyn's insurance wrote us a check for eight thousand dollars! I was so relieved. We made good use of that money. With three girls and a son, we needed the room. We converted our attic into an upstairs for the girls. The Lord has always provided for all my needs in extraordinary ways. I am so grateful to Him for my children. I am so blessed to have them

Adam was around nineteen years old when he began to complain about his stomach hurting. One of my Uncle's happened to be a doctor, Dr. Marshall Ingram, so we took Adam to see Uncle Doc. Uncle Doc was feeling around Adams abdomen during his exam and told us there was something there that should not be there.

He sent Adam for an ultrasound. When we went back he told us that Adam had been born with only one kidney, it was located in the front just below his navel.

As Adam was growing up, I taught him martial arts I also enrolled him in the same martial arts school that I had trained in. He competed all over the country. Adam participated in a martial arts competition held in Colorado Springs during 1996 where he won the World Title in the fighting division.

We had been completely unaware of the damage we had been doing to that kidney.

For eight grueling years, Adam would have to have a stent put in him every six months.

The doctors were brutally honest with us. Eventually, Adams kidney would fail with his only alternative being a kidney transplant to keep him alive. That day finally came.

His kidney suddenly began to completely shut down. Adding to the situation Adam also had an infection.

His mother and I took him straight to Integris Hospital. The doctors there said his kidney would have to come out and he would need to be put on dialysis until a match could be found. Again the hospital room was filled with a quiet intense emotion that only people who have been through such incredible crisis know.

Twenty-two applications were received on behalf of Adam to see if they were a match. They said they had never seen this many donor applicants for one person before. People in El Reno turned out and gave to blood drives specifically for Adam. Both times they had to turn people away because they had no way to keep the blood.

I was a good candidate for a transplant. Fathers usually make a good match for their children. Adam has three sisters and all three stepped up to offer him a kidney. The doctors selected my oldest daughter, Charise to be the one to give Adam the gift of living.

Adam was on dialysis for three months. I have been through and seen many things but never have I witnessed a place so depressing as that. Adam however, would walk around and talk to people before they started his treatment.

He would stop and ask them how they were. He would say,"What is the use in complaining about things?" "Let's try to make the best out of them." The day of the transplant finally arrived. The doctors came out into the waiting room to talk to us.

They said they had good news the transplant could not have gone any better. A wave of relief swept over everyone there. Adam was up and walking within a few hours but his sister Charise was not feeling too good.

As I have said before, the Lord has always provided, He is such a good God. Although I do sometimes question why things happen, He tells me to trust Him no matter what.

I am trusting Him with the writing of this book. It has been eight years since Adams transplant. To look at him now, you would never know a thing has ever happened to him. My daughter, Charise is doing fine to this day also.

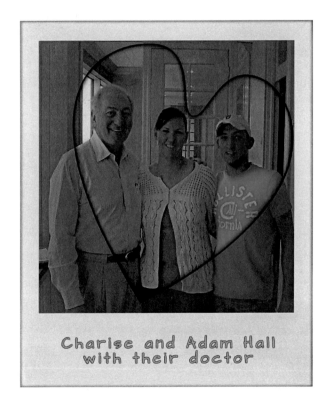

Charise and Adam Hall
with their doctor

Charise and Adam Hall after Adam's kidney transplant during a follow-up visit with their doctor.

9 HOW THE EL RENO
FRIED ONION BURGER DAY COME TO BE

Between 1985 and 1986 the business people of downtown El Reno decided to hire a woman to start a Main Street Program. For those not familiar with the Main Street Program it is a revitalization program started for towns across Oklahoma that help to promote businesses which are located in the downtown historic districts. It offers restoration programs, helps promote events in the town and economic development.

I was not present at the meeting but I was told about it and told that the woman they had hired was named Carolyn. Carolyn was asking the downtown business people what El Reno was most known for.

Almost all of the people at that meeting said it was the fried onion burger. As a result, everyone began to plan an event surrounding the El Reno fried onion burger.Sounds a little bit bizarre doesn't it? An event around a hamburger?

Well, they came up with the idea of cooking the worlds largest fried onion hamburger. They decided it should be held on the first Saturday in May.Here is a little bit of history behind El Reno's fried onion burger. El Reno is called the crossroads of America and that is because it truly is. It is situated at the crossroads of Highway 81 and Route 66.

Prior to there being highways, El Reno was considered a major stagecoach stop and as signs throughout the city point out, part of the Chislom Trail. Texas cattlemen would drive their legendary herds through here on the way to the famous cattle market in Abilene Kansas.

Route 66 was constructed in the year 1926 in order for people to have a standardized way of traveling across the United States. As people traveled through the United States this gave rise to numerous economic opportunities. People needed accommodations like lodging, food, and gas.

Countless people now had opportunities to start small yet profitable businesses along Route 66. One of these was a man named Ross Davis. He ran a place called the Hamburger Inn along Route 66 in downtown El Reno.

Ross invented the onion burger in the mid-1920's during the time of the Great Depression. Just like today, meat was expensive but people needed to eat. So Ross decided to add onions to his hamburgers to cut the cost. He called them Depression Burgers.

Onions were so cheap that it was said Ross would make his hamburgers with half an onion shredded into his five-cent hamburgers. Ross Davis had one of the best locations on Route 66 if you were driving from any direction you would drive by the Hamburger Inn.

When he first started selling these hamburgers smashed with onions people would stop in and pick up sacks of them. So that is how the fried onion burger got its start. Out of necessity during the Great Depression and over eighty years later it still holds its appeal.

As preparations were being made to hold El Reno's Onion Burger Day, Carolyn asked my dad and I if we would be willing to put a grill out on the sidewalk downtown and cook onion burgers. My dad and I agreed we would. We set up our grill between Bickford Ave and Rock Island Ave on the North side of the old Medicine Chest Pharmacy. Carolyn promised me if I would help cook the "big hamburger" that I would get a free Burger Day T-shirt. I remember I really wanted that T-shirt after all this was our first burger day!

The "Big Burger" turned out to weight five-hundred pounds! As my dad and I were setting our grill up to get ready for the day we were not at all sure what to expect. We had prepped three-hundred hamburgers thinking that was pretty good.

Just about the time I had the grill ready to go I could see everyone starting to work on that large hamburger. I told my dad I needed to go help out. At the same time, someone came up to me and asked me if I would cook them some hamburgers.

I did and the aroma of the sweet fried onions on the grill began to circulate through the downtown area. Before I was even finished with the first set someone else walked up and asked me for another order.

The next thing I knew when I looked up I had a line of people that stretched all the way across the street. Our line of people kept growing and growing. Within an hour, I was running out of hamburger meat! By two O'clock my dad was running up to Johnnie's and Otis gave him a pan of hamburger.

It was now going on three O'clock I was getting extremely tired. A man was standing behind me waiting for a hamburger. He was a man I grew up with and had worked with at Johnnie's Grill. His name was Dave Eaton. He asked me how I was doing. So I told him I was getting really tired out there at the pace I was going. I asked him if he would mind cooking some hamburgers for me so I could take a break.

Dave said he would and stepped in for me while I rested. He seemed to really enjoy it. After I was able to rest, I said thank you to Dave got back on the grill and continued to cook my onion burgers.

We would put the hamburger meat on the grill, smash the onions down into the meat then we would turn the meat over so the onions could cook and then put a bun on top of the meat. This is what I had done. The grill was full of hot, steaming, juicy smashed onion burgers.

 I had the buns on top of the meat when this sparrow came flying over my shoulder landing right on top of the hamburger buns! I looked over at my dad and nodded toward the buns pointing at the bird. He just shrugged his shoulders. I didn't know what to do maybe the steam from the onions would obscure him from view.

Quickly I grabbed the little sparrow, hoping no one would see, flung him up in the air and just went on cooking. No one ever did say anything about it. I never did see any feathers either. So, the way I see it everything turned out just fine for the first burger day!

Our first burger day was a great day and a great success. They estimated the turnout in downtown El Reno was around eight-thousand people that day. Our last Burger Day Festival was May 6, 2017, and it was our twenty-ninth year holding this event. This time the hamburger weighed eight hundred and fifty pounds and we had over forty-thousand people visit our little downtown.

I have never seen "The Largest Fried Onion Burger in the World" after the first event. It was so successful that the fire department and police department took over the cooking and care of the hamburger. Main Street takes care of putting out grills and Dave Eden has stepped up to help get it organized and help cook the hamburgers downtown that many people have enjoyed for years.

The whole town participates in Burger Day and everyone who helps has made it what it is. On that day our volunteers put on a large car and motorcycle show, they bring in rides for the children with or local bands performing nearly all the entertainment. It is an experience only a small town can offer, a true feeling of community.

Original Burger Boys of El Reno

Photographer/Ray Dyer

Sid's Diner owner Marty Hall, kneeling center, is helping to bring together the men who helped land El Reno on the map as a national stop for onion burgers. The group gathered last week at Jobe's Drive-in to plan the Feb. 10 meeting of the 'Burger Boys.'

8-12-08

PETE REYNOLDS   LONDON ENGLAND
     "GOD BLESS THE QUEEN"

NICK GOUGH.   YORK. ENGLAND
GREAT BISCUITS ROUTE66 CALIFORNIA OR
                              BUST !!
                                   o o

7/23/09

great bargers!! muts better
holland's bargers!!

greats from holland
-Jolla bakker

Marty Hall

10 REMEMBERING MY DAD

It was the following year the month of July. The hottest month for Oklahoma, with the average temperatures running in the mid-nineties, humidity sometimes well into to the eighty percent or better range which brought the heat index into the triple digits. It was a hot Sunday afternoon when my dad decided he was going to mow the lawn. He went outside and cut the grass not paying too much attention to the heat or how his body would respond.

He didn't realize that his internal body temperature had risen so high he was getting heat stroke until it was already too late.

By the time my dad reached the house he had become one extremely sick man. He had a throbbing headache, was sick to his stomach, his skin was bright red and his breathing had become labored. He ended up staying in bed for three days. My mom finally got him up so she could take him to the doctor for a checkup. The doctor told my dad and mom that he had become dehydrated.

Working in that sun and heat had caused my dad to lose too much fluid which he needed to replace. Later that day my dad came home from that doctor's visit. He still was not feeling right and ended up having a heart attack. My mom picked up the phone and made a distressing call to 911 the dispatcher sent an ambulance.

They transported my dad to the hospital then flew him by helicopter to Presbyterian Hospital in the city. As they were placing my dad in the helicopter I got into my car.

I tried to keep up with the helicopter but there was just no way possible for me to do so. It was too fast which in looking back it was supposed to be and had I kept up with it I might have gotten into an accident.

Everything seemed to move in slow motion. I arrived at the hospital emergency room and they were already preparing my dad for surgery, however, they let me see him for a few minutes. I asked my dad if he was in any pain and he told me he was not. I asked him what the doctor had told him earlier and he said, "He told me I was dehydrated, I needed to drink more fluids and I need to get more rest. I said, "Dad did you tell him you were having chest pains?" He said, "It wasn't anything I haven't felt before." The last things my dad ever said to me was that he loved me. My dad died that night. He died five minutes after midnight on July 7th.

My mom died six years later. She never was able to recover the heartbreak of losing my dad. You could see the pain was something my mom had never experienced. One could not live without the other. They had one of those marriages that surpassed the physical and emotional level. They were truly a pair that had bonded on a deep spiritual level.

Dad was one year from retiring.

I had asked him if once he retired if he would be willing to help me out at the Dairy Hut and if I had another diner if he would help me out there.

He said he would. My dad loved being around people. He would help Otis out at Johnnie's grill in the morning with breakfast. One thing about my dad he sure did like making those onion burgers!

¡Que tal amigos!
Oklahoma, who would have thought? Found my true love & our weeding will be here. Awesome for

Y. A.
Guadalajara, M

11 THE BEGINNING OF SID'S DINER

I was going to work that following April, just like I had done many other days when I pulled up to the stop sign at the corner of Choctaw and Wade streets. For years it had been a vacant corner lot just sitting there, barren in the winter and full of yellow weeds in the summer. You could consider it somewhat of an eyesore. The old El Reno hotel used to sit there before it was decided that it should be moved to the historical district about two blocks down. Now that corner was a big mud hole with some ugly trees.

To me, this was quite sad. I had been used to walking by there on my way to school but like everything, times had changed. I was stopped at that corner when the Lord spoke to my heart. He said, "Son that is your corner if you want it now." It is a hard thing to put into words when the Lord speaks to a Christian. It is not something audible. It is very quiet, very clear and internal.

He will speak to our hearts to feed someone, to help someone financially, to let us know when to hold out tongues, to apologize and to forgive. Over time we begin to recognize when He is speaking to us.

For about a week every time I pulled up to that corner I heard the Lord speak to my heart. Every time He would say,"Son, that is your corner if you want it."

So one day I said," Lord if you are speaking to me I am going to call up and find out if they want to sell it." The couple who owned it lived in Norman and they had bought it as an investment property. I told the Lord if you are really leading me in this than I am going to make an offer of eleven-thousand dollars to these people.

f they accept I will recognize that you are in this.If they turn it down I will recognize that you are not leading me in this direction and I will not pursue this any further.

I went home to call the couple. A man answered the phone. I told him who I was and asked him if he was interested in selling the corner lot in El Reno. He said he was and was asking twenty-five thousand dollars for it. I counter offered and told him I would give him eleven thousand dollars. I could hear him cover the phone receiver with his hand.

Even with his hand over the phone, I was able to hear him speaking with his wife. He was asking her if they would let that lot go for eleven thousand dollars. Her reply was,"Sell it!" Ever since then the Lord has saved me!I had prayed that I would be doing in life what it was He had been calling me to do.

I sat down and began to draw a blueprint up of a diner that I would build on that corner lot. I went out and started to get estimates of what various things would cost. I had some money saved up but it was not going to be enough.

I was going to have to go to the bank. I could clearly see that as I was working on the blueprint. It seemed as if I instinctively knew from the start where everything could go from the water lines to the sewer lines. Where the gas lines should be, the air conditioning and the placement of the electrical wires. It seemed so easy to draw up. As if He was guiding my hand the whole way. Now it was time to take that walk down to the bank. Before I left I told the Lord, if I need a cosigner I am not taking out a loan because you Lord are my cosigner.

I gathered up my blueprints and drove down to the American Heritage Bank on Country Club road. I sat down and talked to the banker and we took a look at my blueprints for the diner. He told me he would call me the next day this was on a Wednesday.

That night I went to church I asked the church f they would pray for me.

I had told banker in the office that I would not have a cosigner in case the business should fail. I did not want to take anyone down with me. The next day I received a phone call from him and he said the bank would give me a loan. He went on to say that in lieu of a cosigner they would need my house, my car, and anything else up front for collateral.

I would need three dollars worth of collateral for every one dollar I was borrowing. I went home and discussed everything over with my wife. We sat and prayed over the situation that this was God's perfect will for our lives.

We had four small children we had put everything on the line. We believed that this was the direction the Lord was leading us in.The bank set me up for a construction loan. How it worked was the money would be given to me by the bank as I needed it. The land had already been paid for so now it was time to start building.

Scotty Higgins had brought in twenty-two truckloads of dirt in order to build the ground up high enough to be able to put a building on the lot.

There are times in a Christians life when the Lord will test just how strong your faith really is. He will watch carefully to see if your faith in Him is strong enough that you will put everything on the line for Him and blindly trust in His guidance and love for you. This was one of those times.

I had already put all my material assets on the line but what I had not figured into the equation was the non-material ones. The things that mattered most to me. My family and friends.

There had been all sorts of talk going around town concerning how I was coming up against Johnnie's and Robert's. Some of it was vicious and created a lot of pressure for me. It was never in my head to be in competition with Johnnie's or Robert's.

One particular piece of gossip was shared with me that stuck in my mind.

Marty Hall

An unnamed source told me that both Johnnie's and Robert's were going to run me out of town. Otis was like a second father to me, I had sold him the Dairy Hut so I had no income coming in. We were on good terms as far as I knew. Everything was on the line with this new diner. Words can be insidious and like poison, they can consume you if you let them.

I had hired a man by the name of Preston Durum to build the frame for my diner. The day Preston arrived on the site with the material to start building, I have to admit, I was scared to death. In my mind, I was thinking, if he goes through with this I could lose everything.

As Preston starts walking up to me, I can remember stepping onto some pretty dark dirt clods that day, as I wrestled with whether or not I should continue with this project.

As I was at a point where I really could back out leave everything the way it was and not do anything right now. Preston is now standing in front of me and he asks,"Where do you want to start?" I looked Preston in the eye and said,"Preston, I am not too far. I can back out." Preston asked me," Have you prayed about it?"

I told Preston, "My whole Christian life I've been praying and the Lord has always lead me where He wanted me." Preston looked at me and said,"Well then quit worrying about it and let's do it!" I looked at the ground where we were standing and said,"Start right here." Preston stuck a welding rod into the ground and that is where we began building Sid's.

Two weeks after this I received a call from my Uncle Bob. Uncle Bob was my dads younger brother. Uncle Bob was an executive at Chevron Oil Company in Baytown Texas.

He asked me if he could step into my dad's shoes and help me run this diner. Uncle Bob was a company man, so I said to him, Uncle Bob you have never had a callous on those hands in your life! He laughed when I said that but told me that he would like to come back to Oklahoma. He had been battling cancer for three years now. I told him I didn't know if the diner would be able to support two families but I would be willing to give it a try.

Uncle Bob moved up here and lived with me for several months. I can say that I am so glad he came up here to help me with this diner! Several other men also helped me work on the diner. Mike Connor, Tom Curtis, Joe Connor, Harold Welliver and others would come by and help out from time to time.

Adam was six years old when I was building the diner.

I remember him wanting to help so I would give him little projects to do like painting something here or there. The day we poured the drive through concrete I had Adam put his name and hand print in it. All in all, it took three months to build that diner.

On the day I opened the doors to Sid's Dinner I had three-hundred dollars to my name. The Lord was faithful and He provided for my family. As I write this book the diner has been open for twenty-seven years. I give all the glory and praise to my Good Shepherd.

When I was building the diner people would always ask me what I was going to call it. My response was always the same. I didn't know yet. I had a few names in mind but I really wanted to name it Sid's Diner. Then I would think if it failed I didn't want to embarrass my dad's name.

Marty Hall

I was working at the diner one day when my mom stopped by. She told me that she had finally removed my dad's name off of everything. As we were talking I asked her if it would be alright if I named the diner after my dad. She told me she thought that would be a fine idea. So that is the story behind how Sid's Diner got its name.

Over the years Sid's Diner has retained the same look and feel of a good old fashioned mom and pop joint after which it was originally designed

Behind the counter at Sid's Diner

George Motz featuring Sid's Diner in Hamburger America.

-8-08
Just like the book (Hamburger America) said!!
Steve & BJ White
Juneau, Alaska

Marty and Adam Hall

Marty Hall

12 FULL CIRCLE

The diner has been open for about twenty years now and I have been cooking hamburgers for close to forty-five years. I often get asked how many burgers I think I have cooked over the course of my career. Usually, I respond with, "A whole lot." One day I decided I was going to sit down and try to figure out as close as I could the number of hamburgers I have actually cooked through the course of my life.

The number came out to nearly five million!

A friend of mine Doug came into the diner and sat behind me at the counter after this. He asked me this question and this time I had the answer. When I gave him the answer of five million he pulled out a piece of paper a pen. He then asked me how many hamburgers make up one pound of meat and started writing.

When he was all done writing he looked up at me and said, "Marty do you know how many cows you have cooked?" Of course, my response was, "No I don't know." Doug said," You have cooked over four thousand head of cattle." I told him jokingly, "I think you have left a zero off of that!" He replied," That is a lot of cattle."

In the year 2011, I began to have a lot of pain in my right hand. At times it would be so bad that I could hardly hold the spatula. About all I was able to do was wash the dishes.

I went to a specialist and was told he could keep my wrist from getting worse but it was not going to get any better. When I asked the doctor about my wrist getting worse he told me if I did not quit cooking hamburgers it was going to just get worse. At this point, I thought my days of flipping burgers may well be over.

One evening about a minute before closing, two men came into the diner a father and son. The son was between the ages of thirty to thirty-five and the father was between the ages of sixty-five to seventy. They sat down placed an order and ate their meal. When they went to pay I asked them if everything was alright and they said yes they had enjoyed their meal.

I don't remember how the subject of my hand came up in the conversation exactly. The younger gentleman asked if he could take a look at my hand. I extended my arm so he could see my hand. With his index finger, he touched my wrist. I almost fell to the floor the pain was excruciating. He said he was sorry about that and followed up with this is really bad. I told them I knew and that I had already seen a doctor and was told there was nothing they could do about it.

It turned out this young man worked in the medical field. Mike Pflughoft, PA-C and he said he knew someone who could fix my hand. The next day he brought me some medicine and some other things which I now don't recall and gave me the phone number for a Dr. Kristopher Avant. I couldn't believe that a doctor would drive all the way back to El Reno to bring me some medicine!

I called Dr. Avant's office and Mr.Pflughoft had already made me an appointment. I showed up for my doctor's appointment was taken back to the waiting room and was sitting there patiently waiting for the doctor to show up.

Marty Hall

When Dr. Avant comes in the first thing he says is, "I know you! My wife worked for you when she was in high school." I asked what her name was and he told me. She is now a doctor. I about fell off the table in astonishment I could hardly believe it. The Lord truly has a way of putting the right people in your path just when you need them. Who would have ever thought at the time that all these years later I would be sitting in front of a surgeon whose wife, now a doctor had once worked for me as a teenager!

Dr. Avant asked to see my hand. I held out my arm so he could take a look at it. He "Well, Marty I have to tell you this is pretty bad," he said. "You are going to need surgery." His office scheduled the day for me to have surgery at the Bone and Joint Hospital in Saint Anthony's. I can say that I was not looking forward to surgery but I was no longer in a

position to bargain it had to be done. I was scheduled for a follow-up appointment one-week post-op. I showed up for my appointment and again stretched out my arm for him to take a look at my hand. After he finished looking at everything he needed to he told me that my hand was healing up pretty well. He then advised me to not be picking up anything heavier than a coffee cup.

Then he shook his finger at me to reinforce what he had said saying," I mean it, Marty, I mean it! Don't go down to that diner for about four weeks." I told him I understood and we finished up our visit.

Anybody that knows me is aware that I simply cannot stay away from the diner for very long. It wasn't too long before I couldn't help but go down and see how things were going and just visit with everyone. I notice that two of my customers have coffee cups that are empty. I walk over to where we have the coffee intending to get the coffee pot so I can refill their coffee cups like I would normally do. As I went to pick up the coffee pot the only thing I could see in my mind's eye was Dr. Avant shaking his finger in my face. I decided it was better not to pick that coffee pot up. I said goodbye to everyone opened the door walked outside got into my truck and drove home.

At my six-week appointment, Dr. Avant looked at my hand and gave me a clean bill of health. He told me I was free to go! When people ask I tell them what he says, I am free to go and do whatever I want. I am so grateful to those two men. Without them, I would not be able to do what I enjoy in my life. I am able to flip burgers and visit with my customers again.

We were pretty busy during lunch hour one day when a young man around twenty-three to twenty-seven years of age came walking into the diner. He sat down on the first bar stool which is right in front of the cash register. I turned around to him to say hello and make some friendly conversation. I asked him where he was from and he told me he had come from Florida. I took his order and went back over to talk with him for a bit.

I have always enjoyed visiting with my customers, asking them what brings them into Sid's Diner and hearing their stories. Whatever it is I am doing I want to keep doing it! This particular young man said he was traveling down I-40 looking for a place to eat. He decided this looked like a nice friendly place so he pulled over here.

 I asked him where he was traveling to. He said he really didn't know. He went on to say he had a major decision to make in his life.

His decision was whether or not he should go into the ministry or to stay in the private sector. I began telling this young man about my story behind Sid's Diner. How the Lord spoke to me about this place, how stepping out and following the Lords call can be very challenging. I told him all about my story and walk of faith.

The young man soon stood up to leave and pay his bill. He said to me, "I'll be thinking of you. One more thing, the Lord used you to answer my prayer." Then he turned and walked out the door. I don' know how the Lord answered his prayer if he went into the ministry or the private sector. I just always kept in mind that even the Lord could use someone like me to answer a man's prayer. That was a pretty powerful thing.

13 NO SUCH THING AS COINCIDENCE

Our little diner is busy. From the time we open the doors for breakfast in the morning until we shut off the open sign in the evening people are coming and going. Needless to say, there is not a lot if any, time for idle chit-chat on the phone. I was cooking on the grill as usual when the phone rang.

One of the girls told me I had a phone call so I washed my hands and took it in the back so I could hear over all the noise in the diner. The person on the other end of the phone said they were calling from the Travel Channel and asked if I had a minute to talk. I said sure.

They told me they were doing a show in Oklahoma called Man V Food with Adam Richman and they were interested in featuring a story on Sid's Diner in an upcoming episode. They were also going to include Cattleman's Steak House and a place called the Steak and Catfish Barn north of Oklahoma City. I told them I would be honored for them to come to Sid's and looked forward to seeing them soon.

We arranged for them to show up on a Saturday. The television crew arrived really early to start setting everything up. Adam Richman didn't get to the diner until around nine O'clock. We nearly bumped into each other coming in. He reached out his hand and said, "Are you, Marty?" I extend mine and with a hearty handshake replied, "Yes sir."

He said," Do you believe a man can eat twenty-nine pieces of catfish?" "I believe you can," to which we both laughed. Adam walked around the diner talking to folks introducing himself to everyone and asking them questions. Everyone was very respectful. I have to say I did enjoy them being there.

Around three o'clock in the afternoon, the crew asked me if I could shut the diner down for a few hours. They explained to me that they needed the diner quiet with no cell phones ringing, no ice cream machine running in the background and no people talking. I told them I understood and no problem. So we closed the diner down for a few hours that afternoon. Having the Travel Channel visiting your diner is not a commonplace event after all.

Marty Hall

Filming of Man VS Food

While the crew was outside getting ready to shoot the next segment Adam and I were sitting at the counter. When you come into Sid's one of the first things you will notice is that I have pictures everywhere. My counter is covered with pictures dating back to the 1800's forward detailing the history of my family, friends and the history of El Reno. I handmade my countertops carefully placing each picture then pouring a clear coat resin over them. The idea was to preserve the history of our town and allow people to come in overtime be able to bring their kids and grand-kids inside the diner point to a picture and say that was your uncle or aunt. I also did this to all my tables.

I have only one picture of Hub Reed, from my high school days, in my entire countertop. Adam picked a seat at the bar and began to tell me a story about his bar mitzvah. Let me tell you that was one funny story to hear Adam tell it. When he finishes telling me his story he looks at the pictures underneath the countertop he spots the picture of Hub Reed. He looks a little closer at that picture points to it and says, "That's Hub Reed!" I nodded my head yes. He went on to tell me how he had watched him play basketball when Hub played for the New York Knicks. New York loved Hub Reed! Hub had been my driving instructor and the Dean of Boys at El Reno High School. We all knew he had played professional basketball but Hub never really talked much about it. He was a man who always focused on the present.

I was about to learn just how good at professional basketball Hub Reed truly was! Adam continued his story, "Did you know Hub could keep Wilt Chamberlin in the single digits?" "Really?!" I replied with some disbelief. "Yep, in Wilt's autobiography of all the players, he didn't like to play with Hub was one of them." You always hear that phrase, "It's a small world". Well on this day there was no room left for doubt there was.

Out of two hundred, some odd pictures on my counter and another nearly four hundred in the diner and Adam sits down in front of the only single picture of Hub Reed in the entire place and tells me an incredible story about a man I have known my whole life that Saturday afternoon!

The next day I just had to call Hub. In high school, his wife Rosa was my typing teacher. Typing was never a strong suit for me and I might have reached ten words a minute on a good day in class. When I had Hub on the phone I asked him if he had ever seen Man V Food and he said he had not.

I started to tell Hub the story about Adam Richman when he interrupted me and asked me if I thought this man was Jewish. I told him I know he is Jewish! Then I explained the story of the bar mitzvah when I had finished I asked Hub why he would ask that particular question. Hub said that when they used to play basketball at Madison Square Garden they would leave the locker and go down to the court. When they got to the court there were people everywhere and among those people was a small group of boys who were Jewish.

He said he would go over and talk to them and autograph their books for them. He said, "Marty I bet you he is one of those boys." I told him I didn't know if he was or not but one thing I did know was that he had left quite an impression on him.

During that phone conversation, Hub went on to tell me a few more stories about his time in New York. One of my favorite stories was about Hub playing basketball; it took place here in El Reno when he was in high school.

El Reno High School looks the same today as it did in when it was first built in 1911. As a matter of fact, it is on the U.S. National Register of Historical Places.

Hub Reed only played basketball one time in El Reno and he told me as he was coming down the side court when he spotted a dime. When he got closer to that dime he bent down and picked it up.

He said a dime was worth a lot back then and he wasn't going to pass it by. What Hub didn't know was that someone had held that dime over a cigarette lighter until it was red hot. When Hub reached down and picked that dime up it burned his fingers and good!

During our conversation, I asked Hub straight out if he really kept Wilt Chamberlin in the single digits. He said to me," Marty one time I did. It was during college and Wilt was sick." Nobody could keep Wilt Chamberlin in the single digits!

The next day I called our local newspaper and spoke to them about the story concerning Adam Richman, Hub Reed, and Wilt Chamberlin.

The paper decided to do a story on Hub how he came to El Reno along with his wife Rosa and how they had served the community as teachers for so many years. I can't think of two any more deserving people.

They were wonderful teachers and inspirations to many young people over the course of their careers while serving the community of El Reno.

14 THE WALL

When you walk through the glass door and into Sid's diner with its red and black décor straight to the right side of the grill there is a wall full of pictures. This wall is full from the top down of pictures of our service men and women through the decades who have fought for our Country. I started this wall a very long time ago. It is my tribute to all who have honored America by ensuring we have the freedoms we do today.

Over the years I have operated Sid's diner I have had more than my share of young men and women enlist in the military. I would always ask them if I could have a picture of them so I could put it on my wall.

Over time this wall has come to have so many pictures of our veterans from El Reno on it that there is barely any room. We always manage though to find a spot and shuffle things around to find a place for one more.These pictures start from World War One and go straight through to today. Every single picture has a story to go with it. On my wall, I have only two pictures that are connected. All the rest are single.

This picture is of Joe Riley Jr. and Jack Hodgkinson Jr. The reason I have these two pictures connected is that Joe Riley was the seventh man from El Reno to be killed in the Vietnam War.

Joe Riley

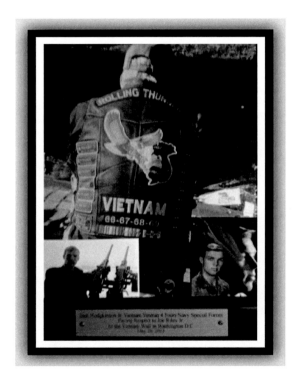

The picture of Jack Hodgkinson shows him visiting the Vietnam Memorial pointing at Joe's name. Jack ended up serving four tours in Vietnam and I have known him all of my life

Another picture I have on my wall is of Alan Ladd. I was going to work one afternoon at Johnnie's Grill when I got there I met Alan Ladd working on the grill. He introduced himself to me and said he had just got home from Vietnam. I really liked being around him. I was able to work quite a bit with him and we enjoyed each others company.

One day I came to work, I remember I was working an afternoon shift, Alan told me he would be leaving in a couple of days. I asked him where he was going off to. He said he had reenlisted to go back to Vietnam. That was not the answer I was expecting.

Dumbfounded I asked him why he was doing that. Alan looked me square in the face he pointed his finger at me and said,"So you don't have to go!" I didn't know what to say. I don't think there is any type of response good enough to that.

Alan Ladd

Alan and I stayed friends over the years. He moved to California and opened a pub.

He would come back and visit El Reno from time to time and we would catch up on things The phone rang and out of the blue Alan had called me up. Before he even said hello the first thing that came out of his mouth was,"have you had a prostate check-up". I said no and he said." go and get it checked." I asked him why and he replied with,"That is an order.". Three months later Alan died of prostate cancer.

I have a picture of my dad on the wall. It is the only picture I have of my dad smiling during his time in Korea. At my dad's funeral, a man walked up to me and he introduced himself as Jim. He told me he had worked with my dad at the Highway Department. As we began to talk he told me that he was a Korean War Veteran. While I was growing up I would always ask my dad to tell me things about his time in the war.

My dad would only tell me two things about Korea. He would tell me how cold it was over there and about this food called Kimchi that the Korean people ate.He would never ever tell me anything more than that.

One time I recalled asking my dad if he ever wanted to see any of his fellow servicemen again, the guys he served with in Korea. Very firmly he said no. I asked him why. He turned his head slightly and said he didn't want to talk about it. I am sure to this day I could see his eyes welling up with tears when he gave me this reply. From that time on I never again asked my dad anything else about Korea.

As Jim and I talked at my dads funeral I learned some things about my dad. My dad had always been a man of integrity but I never knew how much until this day.

Jim told me about an incident that happened in Korea with my dad which he and my dad had talked about.

It brought clarity to why my dad never wanted to revisit his memories of Korea.

My dad and another soldier were going to a village when this other soldier saw a young Korean woman. This other soldier decided he was going to rape this young woman. My dad held a gun to this soldier and told him you are not going to rape her. Jim said when he asked my dad what happened after that all he would say was that she did not get raped. We do not know the rest of the story like I said after hearing this, I understood more why my dad was the way he was.

I get quite a few comments on my wall dedicated to America's veterans, both men, and women, young and old. I am very proud of this wall and what it stands for. It is dedicated to them and it stands as a symbol that they will never be forgotten and that we are thankful for their service. Their service has given someone like me a choice to flip burgers for a living. Every community in America ought to have a wall dedicated to the men and women in their communities who have served and died on behalf of the United States of America.

SID'S WAR MEMORIAL WALL

15 CONCLUSION

Over all of the years, I have worked I have never been open on a Sunday. I have had too many people to count ask me why I don't open my door for business. Sunday would be a great day for customers; it would bring you a lot of money. This may be true. It may all be well and good but like my mom used to say, "Sunday is the Lord's Day."

I need that day, to sing to Him, to praise Him, to learn about Him and be with His people and. to keep my faith strong like an oak tree. This is so much more valuable than the money I could earn being open. Without my faith I am nothing. The Lord has always provided more than enough.

My wife and children have always told me I need to write down the stories I have spent so many years telling my friends and customers. As I approach close to my time of retiring, after fifty years of flipping burgers, I reflect back on my life and I am fortunate to be able to say I am one of the few people who with all honesty would not change a thing in my life.

I have a loving wife who has stuck beside me through thick and thin. I am so proud of all of my children.

My oldest daughter Charise is a paralegal at Miller Dollar Hide, Christa owns Sid's diner in Minco, Oklahoma, my other daughter Sonya owns a diner called Marty's in Arkansas and one day I will hand over Sid's to my son Adam.

I have thirteen grandchildren and I am equally proud of all of them. I have three great-grandchildren which I never thought I would live long enough to see them! If I behave myself I just might live long enough to see a great- great grandchild or two.

Not too long ago a woman I went to school with named Beth came into the diner with her mother. They are another really great family I have known. She asked me how I was doing and I answered fine I have a Good Shepherd. She said I know he likes to watch you flip those burgers! I had never thought of that before, that I, as a burger flipper all my life, could put a smile on God's face.

As someone else recently said to me,"Even God likes a hamburger."

Thank you for this
good union burger lunch

We enjoyed it very much.
'Het was lekker!'

Gerrie + Miranda
3.27.12
The Netherlands

They don't make burgers like this in New York! - we'll be back for more - for sure!
♡ The Mulligans
Apalachin, NY

4/2/12
excellent food! we loved the
milkshakes, thanks!
Sharon + Ed
Stow, Ohio

YOU HAVE NICE PLACE HERE
I ENJOYED HOSPITALKY

CEZARY POLAND

Daniel CZECH

Marty Hall

Carolyn and Marty Hall

Marty Hall and his
wife of many years
Carolyn Hall.

Charise, Sonya and Christa Hall

Marty Hall with his
three daughters

ABOUT THE AUTHOR

Marty Hall was born and raised in Oklahoma. He is married to Carolyn Hall, has four grown children, thirteen grandchildren and a dog named Shorty. Marty has worked in the food industry for over fifty years. He has been self-employed since the age of twenty-one. Marty is also a Born Again Christian.

FOUR SPIRITUAL LAWS

1. God loves people and wants a personal relationship with us

2. For all of us have sinned, and our sin separates us from God

3. The Lord Jesus, God in the flesh died on a cross to wipe away our sin.

4. We must repent of our sins and ask Jesus to forgive us and become OUR SHEPHERD.

As a way of thanking all of the wonderful people who have purchased this book, we would like to offer you the below coupon. Please bring in the original no copies are allowed and it is encouraged, if at all possible, that you bring the book in with it. We greatly appreciate your business as well as how far many of our customers have traveled just to try our food!

God Bless and safe travels,

Marty Hall and all of the Hall Family at Sid's Diner

This coupon is good for one free shake or malt at Sid's Diner in El Reno Oklahoma.

This coupon is not valid at any other Sid's location and is an exclusive promotion for purchasing A Burger Boy on Route 66. This coupon has no cash value.

Notes

Marty Hall

Made in the USA
San Bernardino, CA
26 December 2017